How To Harmonize One's Own

Magnetic Currents

Abby A. Judson

Kessinger Publishing's Rare Reprints

Thousands of Scarce and Hard-to-Find Books on These and other Subjects!

- Americana
- Ancient Mysteries
- Animals
- Anthropology
- Architecture
- Arts
- Astrology
- Bibliographies
- Biographies & Memoirs
- Body, Mind & Spirit
- Business & Investing
- Children & Young Adult
- Collectibles
- Comparative Religions
- Crafts & Hobbies
- Earth Sciences
- Education
- Ephemera
- Fiction
- Folklore
- Geography
- Health & Diet
- History
- Hobbies & Leisure
- Humor
- Illustrated Books
- Language & Culture
- Law
- Life Sciences

- Literature
- Medicine & Pharmacy
- Metaphysical
- Music
- Mystery & Crime
- Mythology
- Natural History
- Outdoor & Nature
- Philosophy
- Poetry
- Political Science
- Science
- Psychiatry & Psychology
- Reference
- Religion & Spiritualism
- Rhetoric
- Sacred Books
- Science Fiction
- Science & Technology
- Self-Help
- Social Sciences
- Symbolism
- Theatre & Drama
- Theology
- Travel & Explorations
- War & Military
- Women
- Yoga
- *Plus Much More!*

We kindly invite you to view our catalog list at:
http://www.kessinger.net

CHAPTER XVL.

HARMONIZING ONE'S OWN MAGNETIC CURRENTS.

Before we take up the processes by which we may put our physical and spirit body into harmony with the currents of magnetism, we have to remind the reader of two things.

One is the unity prevailing through the whole earth sphere, so far as the forces of nature are concerned. By the earth sphere, we mean not only the physical planet, but also the whole of its spirit world, extending far beyond the moon. The latter, having been brought into form by a whirl of its own, said whirl being subordinate to the far larger one that brought the earth into sensible form from the cosmic ether, the moon is thus a part of the earth sphere, just as the latter is in its turn a part of the solar one. The earth sphere is therefore a unit, so far as what is beyond it is concerned, and all the beings living in its different parts are connected to each other in a way that they are not connected to beings living beyond it. Whether any of us be ever brought into immediate and sensible communication with those of planets beyond will depend solely on our having first used all the means of development pertaining to the terrestrial sphere to which we belong.

We who are in our fleshly bodies now are just as much members of the spirit world of the earth as those who have dropped the fleshly body. We are spirits now, in these bodies, and where we are now is the lowest sphere of the spirit world of the earth. It is here that we take up the thread of individual, conscious existence, though the infinite life out of which we were born has always been. To our mind, the most amazing thing about the formation of entities is that out of the infinite fountain are ever coming new ones, each endowed not only with individual consciousness, but with what metaphysicians call "the power of contrary choice." This fact, which we must accept, because it is fact, is easily accepted, if we bear in mind what the nature of infinite power must be, and what it can therefore do.

On this plane do we come into conscious being, and, once done, the act is not repeated by any one individual, so far as being actually born again is concerned. In the present imperfect development of our whole sphere, nearly all who pass out of the physical body will still have lessons to learn on this plane. They will linger near, they will share our doings, our sufferings, our experiences, in connection with us. They will even take control of a physical body temporarily, while its normal tenant is psychologized by its own attendant spirits. When in these and similar ways its physical development has been completed, it will not return to this plane, only as it seeks to benefit mortals. When the whole earth sphere has reached its full development, this partial return will not be necessary. Each will fully get what it needs in its earthly sojourn before passing out of the fleshly form, and in each will be realized Milman's beautiful lines regarding the ascension of the Nazarene:

"Then calmly, slowly wilt thou rise
    Into thy native skies,
Thy human form dissolved on high
    In its own radiancy."

To that time do we look, and towards that consummation do all our energies bend.

We would next earnestly remind the reader that the physical processes of harmonizing with the currents of the earth sphere should not be attempted until the first part of the book, the part that relates to harmonizing the soul with the higher intelligences, has been fully comprehended and accepted. It were better not to develop magnetism at all in the outward forms than to do so while leaving the development of the soul at the same time unattended to. On this rock has many a medium found his bark wrecked, and ages of his spirit life may be expended in the long struggle to make up his sad neglect while here. Just as the wise man will "eat to live" and not "live to eat," so the wise aspirant to higher conditions will make the development of his magnetic (mediumistic) development wholly subordinate to the unfoldment of his soul.

If human beings ever become wholly magnetic, in perfectly harmonious surroundings, they will not then need processes to regain harmony. . But not having yet attained such a condition permanently, we still need to employ ways and means, though it is very likely that further progress may allow the practice of these methods to take place at longer intervals.

We will suppose a case, alas! the very condition of too many, and the condition of the writer prior to her development. Of this person we may say that his individual being is out of harmony with the magnetic currents of the whole earth sphere, and he does not always feel well. He becomes nervous and excited when his cares multiply on him. Once, he could sleep in spite of care, but now laying his head on the pillow seems to bring his troubles more vividly before his mind. Like the evil messengers to Job, while one trouble stares him in the face, another comes to mind, and before that is fairly faced, yet another appears before him, till his head throbs, sleep flies far away, and he sits up in bed staring at the wall "like a well-bred maniac," a prey to ten-fold cares, any one of which is enough to distress a human being. That he is their prey is literally true. He is their victim. They have their way with him wholly, and he cannot resist. Perhaps he does not sleep at all; and, if he does so, these cares become embodied in painful forms or disastrous events in his dreams, and he rises in the morning to fight the world, or to succumb to leaden-eyed despondency. His nervous condition makes him irritable, and liable to disease. Perhaps he is a Spiritualist, and knows that spirits return to bless some persons, but he has personally no sense of their presence. If he knows nothing of these things, God seems afar off, and not at all like a father, and even his loved ones here seem to have changed. Alas ! for the millions in our country who are in these hard conditions, especially since the multiplication of monopolies has increased so grievously the burdens of the poor ! And the millionaire is perhaps no happier than the poor man. Having money does not make him magnetic, and his physical and mental gearing is out of order.

Harmony with one's environment is what he needs,

and as we are now on the physical part, we will give the first step in the physical process. The object of this first step is to throw off one's present personal magnetism, in order afterwards to replace it by that which is in harmony with the whole earth sphere

In a former part of the book, we spoke of the earth being a magnet itself; and though this is equally true of the whole earth sphere, including its spirit world, we direct our attention now to the physical planet on whose surface we now dwell. Being a magnet, it is in polarized condition, and most scientists call the north end of it positive and the south negative. French savants, with the same accuracy which leads them to measure a piece of ribbon by the forty-millionth part of the earth's circumference through the poles, call the north pole of a magnet its negative end, and vice versa, because it is the positive end of a free magnet that turns to the north. We should be inclined to say that the north pole of the earth is its negative end; and therefore the positive end of a magnet, its north end, as most nations call it, turns, when free, to the north.

In accordance with the fact that the particles of coarser matter are borne to the axis between the poles by the force of the whirl that formed the earth, we see that the denser particles go towards the negative pole, thus perhaps causing the great continents to greatly predominate in the northern hemisphere.

But while the mind eagerly seeks the true cause and explanation of things, our real object is to show what the process is by which a person may throw off his desultory and inharmonious magnetism, preparatory to harmonizing himself, leaving it to others to show how this actually effective process may be explained by their theory regarding terrestrial magnetism.

For some reason that must be found in the actual laws of nature, *because* our act produces the effect desired, we stand (if not disabled) facing the north pole of the earth. We do this wherever we may be, because it is the earth as a whole that is a magnet. As we wish to throw off our cross magnetism, we first take it under control by drawing it towards our person by any movements that seem conducive to that end. The writer finds it best to collect her magnetism to herself by motions with her hands and arms. The arms, with the back of the hands uppermost, are raised, and sweep the magnetism towards the body by successive downward movements. The hands as well as the arms participate in this act. If we make only these movements, we should be ever concentrating our personal magnetism, without getting rid of it in the slightest degree. So, while we are drawing it within our control, we must at the same time do something to throw it away from the body. This is accomplished by slowly turning around *to the left* two or three times, while continuing all the while the movements of the arms described above.

Of course, most readers will at once inquire *why* turning to the left makes the magnetism leave the body. And yet, (may I say it?) I had practiced this for years without ever asking why I turned to the right or left, doing it because I was bid to do so; and it was only when I began to teach others, many of whom asked this question, that I was led to think of it. Whether it was stupidity or receptivity on my part, I do not know. I say this in humility and candor.

Pardon my using the homely old proverb, "The proof of the pudding is in the eating." What I do know is that I never heard of any such processes till I was fifty-two years of age, and that I at once began to practice them according to the physical directions laid down in this book. Soon the mental part grew on me, till it developed to what has previously been expressed. Before beginning this process, I had no mediumship that I knew of, though it was latent in me, as in all. By this process, I have become clairvoyant enough to see many spirits when alone, especially those dearest to me; to sometimes hear them speak to me; to be frequently impressed by them in my mind; to feel my mother's caresses and my father's embrace. Besides these precious personal experiences and hundreds more, I have by following these directions become enabled to often give extempore lectures in public. Once so timid that I could not speak a word in a prayer-meeting without holding onto something, I can now face any audience without fear. Also, I am enabled to work for the spirit world, having learned how to put myself, *at will*, into condition to write a book as large as this in less than five weeks. It goes to the printer in first copy, just as written originally, barring the alteration of a word or so, or some change in punctuation. It is true that I am not writing for literary praise or perfection. I am just using this avenue to communicate to those who desire to know what has proved so beneficial to me, in the hope of forwarding the "latter day glory" foretold long ago.

Of course there is a reason in nature's laws for turning to the left when throwing off magnetism, and for turning to the right when centralizing one's own forces. All this will be explained by scientists, as this process is found to produce the desired effects in many persons, and to be thus accordant with these laws.

Mankind used the polar star to guide their path, nobody knows how many thousand years before it was ascertained that it was no more stationary than the equinoctial star. They trusted the polar star, and committed themselves to its guidance, and did well in doing so, though their explanation of natural reasons was far astray.

For myself, when I am going to throw off, I face the north (which I take to be the negative pole, though that matters not), draw my magnetism under control with the movements of my arms, and as I turn round and round to the left, I *can feel the magnetism leaving my body*.

What has just been described is the first physical step. Having gotten rid of that previous, mixed, inharmonious, and disagreeable condition, I am now prepared to receive new, harmonious magnetism from the great earth magnet ; or, in perhaps better words, to put myself in harmony with its currents, by putting my body in the position that will best conduce to this result.

Having been careful during the first step to constantly turn toward the left, never interrupting the process of throwing off by turning the least in the opposite direction, we come at its close into quiet equipoise, as we find ourselves at the beginning of the second physical step, facing the south pole of our great mother magnet.

It is a law with these currents that when two of them

are free to move, they seek to become parallel. We, too, are small magnets, each in himself, and being now clear and free, our personal currents may begin to harmonize with those of the earth itself.

Let us, then, so dispose ourselves that the currents of this small human magnet may most easily become parallel with those of the immense magnet on which it is placed. I face the south, that being the direction from which the currents emanate with which I desire to assimilate. That this magnet may be as free as possible, I not only stand, but I rest on the balls of my feet, rather than on the back of the foot. It is noticed that inspirational speakers naturally stand thus, this position gracefully expressing our aspiration towards something higher. Desiring to blend with the currents from that direction, I bow the head a little towards the pole, and close my eyes in order to shut away outside and diverting influences. As it is to the south that 1 look for the life-aiding currents, I stretch my arms and hands to the south. I keep the fingers apart, as every finger acts as a wire for the conduction of the currents. I keep my hands apart, and am thus a small horse-shoe magnet, one hand being its positive pole, and the other its negative.

While the above attitude, being in accordance with all the facts of the case, is the best one that can be taken at this stage of the process, we cheerfully admit that many persons can assimilate themselves with the earth currents in some other position. One *might* do it, facing the east; but one does it more easily, facing the south. The end might be attained sitting down, but less readily than in the way that has been indicated. No doubt the second step may be done just as effectively in a recumbent position, with the head to the north, and the hands, in free air, stretched towards the south. This is especially recommended to one who is in the practice of this process, when he finds himself unable to sleep. But in the general practice, which includes the five successive steps, it is more convenient to stand during the second step.

I have often been asked how long one should stand while thus harmonizing his body. There can be no definite time the same for all. The same person may continue this second step a longer time on one occasion than on another. One should certainly not stand till tired, nor continue standing when any unpleasant feelings come. From a minute to perhaps three would be right. But we advise all to let their watches and clocks wholly alone in these processes. Waves of magnetism and soul waves are not to be measured off by the ticks of any earthly chronometer. Personal feelings, and the impressions made on one's brain by those disembodied friends who desire to aid our progress, will soon guide us aright, if our motives be aspirational.

While engaged in the second step, some persons feel a tingling in their hands, or a thrill along the back, the first time they try the process. Others may have to keep it up for months before perceiving any effect at all. The latter was the case of the writer. Being quite out of magnetic harmony through a long course of severe labor in the exercise of her profession as a teacher, though very magnetic, and thus successful in what she undertook, she felt no currents at all. But as she believed in the method, and was willing to try anything however hopeless that might bring her into rapport with the spirit world, and doubtless urged to perseverance by the persistence of her spirit friends, she kept on; and at last, after months, she began to feel thrills of magnetism along the nerve centers of the back, when engaged in the second step. At the present time, she cannot go through the process without experiencing the same in a marked degree; and many times when reading, speaking, or thinking, she feels the same, and realizes that invisible ones are seeking to impress some thought or feeling on her brain. The thrill is magnetic, as is proved by its being exactly the same as the quiet current that one feels when holding the ends of a magnetic belt that have been dipped in acid. Experiencing this frequently, and being easily influenced thus by the disembodied, shows a considerable advance from what she was when beginning this exercise.

She has thus related her own experience in this particular, in order to encourage those who, like her, feel nothing when they first begin. Let such take courage, and recollect that during the time they feel nothing, they are still being prepared, if they persevere, for the condition when they will sense the magnetic currents, and will surely succeed in the end if they keep on.

To recapitulate, we have in the first step thrown off all inharmonious, personal magnetism; in the second, we have sought to blend that of our own little magnet with that of the terrestrial sphere. We are now, if successful, in a magnetized condition, every atom of our corporeal frame, both the fleshly and the spiritual, being polarized, and vibrating in harmony with our far-reaching environment. As high disembodied spirits are in the same condition, we may now appropriately invoke their assistance, because they can now reach us. They could not reach us freely before we were thus magnetized, however desirous they were of doing so. Let us now describe the physical part of the third step.

The second one had us standing facing the south, having reached that position by turning to the left. From this point, we turn no more to the left, but wholly to the right, because we are now harmoniously magnetized, and of course desire to retain that condition as long as possible. So, at the close of the second, we turn to the right till we again face the north. and are now completely ready to take the third.

We raise our hands towards the part of the spirit world that is above us, because it is from beyond the earth plane that we expect our help. We also look with uplifted head and open eyes in the same direction. We do not need to cringe and bow, in fear and terror. We look up with all the confidence of a child who knows that he is loved. In this attitude, we think of the power and life of the universe, of the Infinite Intelligence that pervades all. Having attained the consciousness of our share in the all-pervading force, and of our oneness with the infinite life, we make the invocation that was given on page 72. While making the invocation, which we give audibly or silently as suits our feeling, we turn clear round once to the right, with our hands and eyes still uplifted. That brings us again facing the north, and the third step is completed. There should be no pause between the third and fourth step. Having thrown off all inharmony, having become magnetized, and having received aid from above, the result of being in full rapport with God and the angels, we *at once* proceed to take full possession of our own magnetic sphere, in the fourth step.

It will be remembered that in the second one we drew our magnetism towards us, preparatory to throwing it off, and that we brought it to our body by certain movements of the hands and arms. We now make the same movements that serve to bring our magnetism within our own control, but instead of throwing it off by turning to the left, as in the second step, we now *turn to the right*, while making the same movements with the arms and hands, and thus gather and concentrate all the available force within our own sphere.

It is by no means selfish to do so, for thus doing we detract nothing from those about us. In fact, the available strength of all who thus do is greatly increased, both individually and by the union of their forces. High spirits do the same, or they are continually in the same powerfully magnetized condition, without going through the set processes of renewal which are needful for those on the earth plane at the present stage of human advancement. Spirits that we may call highly developed when venturing to compare them with ourselves are not only very strong as individuals; but, by the great harmony mutually prevailing, they unite their forces and can accomplish results that old-time thinkers presumed only a god could accomplish. May it be suggested that even the mighty forces by which the cosmic ether is made to whirl, preparatory to the formation of a new system of worlds, may be brought into action by many individual and powerful spirits who, in perfect harmony, work to the same end? By such a suggestion, we by no means would imply that the existence and acts of such mighty spirits militate against a force far beyond them, which we may call, for want of a better term, the infinite power. Ah! no: the greater the power and the acts of finite intelligences, incomparably beyond them is that which is wholly absolute, unconditioned,— the all and in all!

But let us return to the fourth step, where, as previously described, we turn round and round three or four times to the right, thus wrapping ourselves up in our own magnetic sphere. Thus enwrapped, nothing uncongenial to us can penetrate it. A person may touch us physically, but if we are thoroughly wrapped up, he cannot affect us magnetically.

Our magnetic sphere is said to extend some twelve feet beyond us in every direction—above, around, and even below—for the earth and material objects are permeable by magnetism. When we say that this personal sphere is some twenty-four feet in diameter, we mean that our individual magnetism easily reaches so far. Of course persons may be within this radius who are wholly unable to affect it. We may be so perfectly enwrapped that we shut him out completely. A skilled magnetic healer understands this. He can "shut himself up," as one expressed it, and prevent the streams of his magnetism from reaching one whom he does not wish to reach, while directing them in all their beneficent power upon the one he desires to heal.

A great orator has great magnetic power. Endowed with a physique easily permeated by it, he creates around him a sphere that is powerfully felt by sensitive persons. While his own concentrated sphere does not individually extend through the space of a large audi-

torium, he can easily reach an immense audience. This
is done by the aid of persons who are present. If his
nearest hearers were some two hundred feet away, he
could not affect them easily, though his voice were amply
sufficient. Magnetic hearers, who are personally within
his magnetic sphere, and who are interested in what he
says, have their own currents which blend harmoniously
with his own, and enlarge his sphere. Others beyond
are enfolded in the same, till the whole audience is
melted into a harmonious unit of eager listeners, and he
sways them at his will.

I have heard that the famous and philanthropic
woman orator of Kansas remarked that she did not like
to be on too high a stage, because it made her magnetism go higher than the heads of her audience. Experi-
enced speakers do not wish their audience, the front ones,
too far away. Most will agree that it is easier to speak
when the nearest ones are not more than twelve feet
away, especially when those who are nearest are in full
sympathy with the subject discussed. Clergymen like
to have the front seats occupied. If these are filled they
are indifferent to the rows in the rear. One of the most
spiritual men I ever listened to, a sensitive and magnetic
man, who could thrill a great audience if the conditions
were right, always urged the ushers to fill up the front
pews first. The modern style which substitutes a low
platform for the boxed-up elevated pulpit, and comfort-
able open chairs for the little separate walled in rooms
for the audience, is in accord with the laws of magnetism. Opera-houses and lecture-rooms led the way in
this reform, and the church, as usual (begging its pardon most humbly), followed.

Perhaps some of my readers were visitors at Mr. Beecher's church some twenty-five or thirty years ago. Well do I remember the great audience-room, filled to repletion, with all the space clear to the speaker's stand occupied by seats, which surrounded it, for there were nearly as many persons behind it as in front. Thus encompassed, and re-inforced as it were, was the great orator of humanity. His powerful and generous physique, his great brain, his inspired glance, were all magnetized, and he held the vast throng without an effort. Blue, ministerial, New England blood was in his veins; but a bluer blood, that of generic man, filled them, showing the "heart within blood-tinctured, of a veined humanity." He spoke to man as he was in reality, not as falsely pictured by a mistaken theology. His giant shoulder gave a mighty push to the car of human advancement.

Beecher helped his audience and his audience helped him. He spoke with them, and not to them. His magnetic and spiritual spheres blended with theirs, and the resulting harmony was a power that was felt to the ends of the nation, and far beyond. His free soul seldom knew hesitation or fear, and he easily heads the long line of American pulpit orators.

One easily recalls the names of those men who have greatly influenced others by powers that were made effective by their magnetism. Moses, Jesus, Demosthenes, Cæsar, Mohammed, Luther, Napoleon, Lincoln, were largely endowed with this easily conducting vehicle of the force within, and show how much can be done with its aid; and how little men are personally influenced by those who repel them, like Justinian, Calvin, and

Erasmus. Other things being equal, it is the magnetic men that are followed, listened to, and that get the votes.

By the third step, our personal magnetism was harmoniously blended with that of the earth; and by the fourth, it is gathered together and is fully under our own sway. The more frequently thàt this occurs, the longer does this effective state continue; but, until complete development be attained, our labors in the outside world and the influence of the inharmonious streams from persons we meet, cause it to dwindle away, and to be replaced by an inharmony that needs a repetition of the entire process. To defer this necessity as long as possible, to lock up our sphere as it were, we now pass to the fifth physical step, which should follow up the fourth without any delay.

In this we lock up the centralized power that we have attained, by passing the fingers of one hand across the palm of the other hand, without touching it. We then reverse the reciprocal action of the two hands, and repeat this alternative action two or three times. The hands being the poles of our personal horse-shoe magnet, these motions tend to hold the physical system in a polarized condition, somewhat as the soft iron armature placed across the ends of a steel magnet causes it to retain its polarity.

In this connection, if we find ourselves in presence of a person who is inharmonious, or who seeks to influence us unduly for self-interested motives, we may concentrate our own magnetic forces, and thus protect ourselves, by quietly putting our feet together, and placing one hand over the other. These motions actually concentrate our magnetic currents, and the act also brings our mind into a more positive state.

In the fifth step, it is better to first pass the fingers of the positive hand across the palm of the negative hand; but this is not essential, if the alternative motions of the hands be repeated two or three times. Some persons find it difficult to decide which hand or which side of the body is positive. The right is generally the positive; but as there are exceptions to this statement, we may say that the hand, the cheek, the wrist that is habitually warmer than the other, indicate that that side is positive, and the cooler, the negative. One may test one's own cheeks, always with the same hand; or have another person test one's hands,—with his same hand, of course, as his own hands differ in temperature from each other.

We have thus described the five physical steps of the process, leaving it to Chapter XVIII to show how to combine them with the mental steps given in previous chapters of the book.

> "Conscious Law is king of kings
> From world to world the Godhead changes,
> Thou meetest him by centuries,
> And lo! he passes like the breeze:
> Thou seek'st in globe and galaxy,
> He hides in pure transparency;
> He is the axis of the star,
> He is the sparkle of the spar;
> He is the heart of every creature,
> He is the meaning of each feature;
>   And his mind is the sky,
>   Than all it holds more deep, more high."
>   EMERSON.

This is the end of this publication.

Any remaining blank pages are for our book binding
requirements and are blank on purpose.

To search thousands of interesting publications like this one,
please remember to visit our website at:

http://www.kessinger.net

LaVergne, TN USA
03 January 2011
210886LV00001B/150/A